Summer of Wild Horses

Summer of Wild Horses

Esther Carleton-Lausten

Review and Herald Publishing Association
Washington, DC 20039-0555
Hagerstown, MD 21740

This book was
Edited by Penny Estes Wheeler
Designed by Dennis Ferree
Cover design by Bill Kirstein
Cover art by Jackie Magee

Printed in U.S.A.

Library of Congress Cataloging in Publication Data

Carleton-Lausten, Esther, 1912-
Summer of wild horses.

Summary: The author recounts a special summer in the 1920s when she and her sisters visited Grandma's Montana farm where they encountered rattlesnakes, rode a variety of animals, and watched Uncle Hank break wild horses.

1. Ranch life—Montana—Juvenile literature. 2. Montana—Social life and customs—Juvenile literature. 3. Carleton-Lausten, Esther, 1912- - Childhood and youth—Juvenile literature. 4. Montana—Biography—Juvenile literature. [1. Farm life. 2. Horses. 3. Montana—Social life and customs. 4. Carleton-Lausten, Esther, 1912-] I. Title.
F731.C36 1988 978.6'032 88-1863
ISBN 0-8280-0422-6

CONTENTS

CHAPTER 1

My sister Gertrude gazed listlessly out the train window as it chugged slowly through the dry North Dakota prairie. Smoke and cinders drifted through the open windows, making the summer day seem even hotter. Trains in the 1920s burned coal, and air-conditioning had not yet been invented. We girls had been riding all day and were beginning to get bored.

All of a sudden Gertrude sat up with a yell. "Hey, look! Wild horses!"

Viola and I jumped off our seats and leaped across the aisle to see. There, thundering off to the west, galloped a band of wild horses, their manes flying in the wind. I loved horses anyway, and those wild ones racing across the prairie, unchallenged by anyone, thrilled me immensely.

Viola, age 12; Gertrude, age 8; and I, age 10, were from Minnesota. Because our father was an engineer on the Great Northern Railroad, we often received free passes to ride some of the trains.

Mama had decided that Vi was old enough to watch us and we were old enough to behave. That's how we found ourselves on a slow train heading toward Montana. We would spend the summer with Grandma and Uncle Henry, out on their ranch. We had other family living in the nearby Montana town of Wibaux.

Having never lived on a farm, we had all sorts of visions of the fun we'd have. Uncle Henry—or Hank, as most of us called him—was a cowboy. He broke horses for neighbors and friends on his ranch. (Breaking a horse means to tame it for riding or pulling a wagon.) Of course, he also raised crops. Grandma had chickens and a big garden to keep her busy.

Getting on the train by ourselves and riding alone like grown-ups had been thrilling, but by late afternoon, after hours of sitting quietly, we were tired. The scenery never changed. Flat prairie stretched as far as the eye could see. There were few trees—just grass, grass, grass. We went through many little towns, and the train stopped at every one of them. We thought we'd never get to Grandma's.

About 7:30 that evening we jumped to attention when the conductor strode through the train calling, "Wibaux, next stop. Wibaux, next stop."

We scurried around getting our suitcases down from the rack, then hurried to the bathroom to wash smoke and cinders from our faces and hands. By the time we'd stopped by the watercooler for yet another drink, the train bumped to a stop.

Aunt Mattie was there to meet us. She hugged us and explained that Uncle Henry couldn't drive the horses at night, so he and Grandma would be after us the next morning. "Your cousins are at a party at the church, so we'll go right over there," she told us.

"Oooh, a party the very first thing," Viola exclaimed. All of a sudden we weren't tired anymore. Aunt Mattie had brought our cousins' coaster wagon for us to haul our suitcases in, and we started down the sidewalk, each taking turns pulling the wagon.

As we drew near the brightly lighted building, we spotted Isabelle, George, and Al inside. The games were almost over, and everyone was getting ready for the refreshments. We almost screamed when we saw that we were going to have ice cream and cake. Electric ice-cream freezers hadn't been invented back then, and it was hard to keep ice cream frozen, so we didn't have it very often.

"Eat it slowly and make it last as long as you can," warned Izzy.

At last the party was over, and we went over to our cousins' and got ready for bed. We discovered that we were tired after all and were anxious for morning to come so we could see Grandma and Hank.

After breakfast the next morning, we all lined up on the porch, watching the road for Grandma and Uncle Henry. Isabelle and George soon tired of watching. "Come on," they told me. "It takes a long time to come in from the country with horses and a wagon. Let's go play."

It was almost noon when we heard the wagon rumbling up the dusty street toward the house. While Henry tied the horses to the fence, Grandma got down from the wagon and hugged and kissed us all. Aunt Mattie had dinner ready, so we went into the house to eat. After the grown-ups had visited for a few minutes, it was time to go.

Grandma, Henry, and Vi sat on the high front seat. Gert and I climbed into the back of the wagon, sitting on the edge with our legs dangling over.

A crack of the whip sent the horses off with a jerk, causing Gert and me to fly off the wagon onto the dusty road. We lay for a moment with our faces in the dirt, wondering what had happened, but soon scrambled to our feet and brushed off our clothes. Henry laughed as if it were a big joke, but Grandma told him to hush and we climbed back onto the wagon again.

I looked at Grandma as we rolled along the bumpy road. She had pulled her silver hair straight back into a bun. A black straw hat perched on top of her head like a saucy bird. A frothy lace collar adorned her plain black dress.

Hank looked like the cowboy that he was. His shabby 10gallon hat shaded his tanned face and covered his curly black hair. A scarlet handkerchief was knotted at his neck. Blue jeans and a plaid shirt completed his costume.

It was his jet-black boots with the jingling silver spurs that fascinated me. How I would love to wear them with the 10-gallon hat and ride a wild horse. Uncle Henry had one at the farm, I knew. A riding horse named Chum. Bouncing there in the back of the wagon, my eyes on Hank's black boots, I decided that I'd ride Chum before the summer was over.

We had a long, hot ride through miles of grassy range. The dust dried our noses and mouths until I thought I'd die without a drink of water. Brown hills surrounded us on all sides and the road wound through and around them. Blue misty mountains faded off in the distance.

The heat beat down upon us in shimmering waves. The acrid scent of the sweating horses drifted back from their gleaming, coppery bodies. "A prairie dog village!" I yelled as we rounded a hill. There before us, as far as we could see, were little moundlike houses. At my holler, chubby little prairie dogs, standing by their holes and chattering among themselves, let out a squeak and vanished into their holes. They popped up again just as quickly, curiosity getting the best of them.

"Can we catch one and keep it for a pet?" Gert asked.

Grandma laughed. "You'd never catch one if you tried. Besides, they're wild and might bite."

Then we spied a graceful coyote standing nearby, watching us pass. "Look, he doesn't even act afraid of us," Vi said.

Hank laughed. "He'd run in a hurry if I stopped the wagon."

"Oh, stop and let us pet him," I pleaded.

"Why? You want to lose a hand?"

Suddenly I let out a shriek, and the horses bolted forward in a run. Grandma and Hank jerked around to see what was the matter, while Hank pulled the horses back into a walk.

"Look! Wild horses—and so close. Will they come to us?" A band of mustangs were racing in the wind, their manes and tails flying. A magnificent black horse stopped and looked our way. He started toward us and I shivered. How close will he come? I wondered. But then, with a snort, he whirled, bucked, and galloped after his mates, now hidden in a cloud of dust.

"I hope someone catches that black one and brings him to you to break," I cried.

Hank laughed again. "Some of those stallions are pretty hard to catch, so don't count on it."

At last we reached the top of a long hill. Vi shouted, "There it is. There's the ranch." Nestled in a valley, the weatherbeaten buildings gleamed silvery in the slanting sunlight.

Grandma quickly got supper ready while Hank milked and fed the cows. Bedtime came early on a ranch that had no electric lights. As I lay in my bed, my thoughts kept whirling. *Will I get to ride Chum? Will I get to milk a cow? Will I see a rattlesnake? Will I get to pet a coyote?* Finally I drifted off to sleep, but not before wondering if Mama was missing her three girls.

CHAPTER 2

We got up bright and early the next morning. Grandma had breakfast ready, and Uncle Hank was out milking the cows. We were ready to dash out to watch, but Grandma held up her hand and told us to sit down. "There are a few ground rules that must be laid out before you can go outside," she said. Her tone told us that she meant business.

"You are used to living in town but things are different here," she began. "In the city you can walk around with your heads in the air, gazing at anything and everything. But you can't do that here. We've never seen a rattlesnake in the yard or barnyard, but that doesn't mean there couldn't be one. Around here you must always be on guard. Rattlesnakes could be anywhere; Uncle Hank finds them in the fields and along the roads. You must learn to watch the ground in front of you at all times, and especially if you're near long grass."

She paused while we wiggled and looked at each other. "Another thing," she said sternly. "Uncle Hank breaks wild horses, and you must never go near them. Don't try to pet them. Don't walk up behind them. They can bite and kick. If you want to watch Hank break the horses, you must be very quiet. One loud shout or laugh could spook a horse and cause a runaway. It could ruin the horse and even cause Uncle Hank to get hurt or killed! You must always watch from something high, like a fence or chicken coop," she went on. "If a horse gets away from Uncle Hank and comes running toward you, he could run right over you if you're on the ground."

I sighed, wishing Grandma didn't sound so serious. "We have a bull named Francis," she told us. "He's never hurt anyone, but you can never trust a bull. If Hank lets you bring in the cows, you stay as far away from the bull as you can. If he's with the cows, he usually follows with no trouble. If he's off by himself, don't try to catch him or lead him. Just leave him alone and let Hank go after him."

Just then Uncle Hank came in with the pails of frothy milk. Grandma strained it and put it in crocks that she placed in the coolest place she could find. When the cream rose to the top, she would skim it off to make butter. Later she'd take some of the butter and some of the eggs from her chickens to town to trade for other needed groceries.

At last we sat down to eat, and our eyes grew big at the breakfast Grandma had made. Oatmeal with raisins and real cream. Fried eggs and toasted homemade bread with fresh butter. Canned peaches from Grandma's cellar, and as a treat, Grandma had baked a cake the morning before.

As we ate, I asked, "Uncle Hank, are you going to break a wild horse today?" I couldn't wait to get to those wild horses.

"No, not today." He looked at me and grinned. "I don't

have one today, but Mr. Connelly said he'd be bringing me one next week."

"What'll we do today?" I wondered aloud.

"You can help me with these dishes," Grandma said, "and then we'll go feed the chickens."

"Can we help gather eggs?" Gertrude asked, her eyes wide.

Grandma smiled at her. "Chickens don't lay eggs at night. You'd better give them all day to lay them. Then you can gather them tonight."

Watching the chickens gobble up the feed as fast as we threw it down on the ground was fun. "Look at them fight over their food as if there weren't enough for any of them," Vi said scornfully.

Grandma nodded. "Yes. They're just like a bunch of kids, aren't they?" Grandma had had 15 children, so she should know.

"I'm going to take you for a tour of the farm," she told us when we'd thrown the last of the chicken feed. "I'll show you where you can play and where you can't."

She led us to the barn, and we went inside. She introduced us to Chum, Uncle Hank's riding horse, and told us that we weren't to try to ride him. "He's not completely tame, and still has a few tricks," Grandma told me. "You could get hurt." As we petted and talked to him, he seemed perfectly tame and I promised myself that I would ride him before the summer was over.

Walking over to the other stalls, Grandma said, "Of course, you already know Bum and Brownie. They brought you home yesterday." Bum and Brownie were nice and tame, so we could get right into their stall and pet their necks and backs.

When we went to the cow barn, Uncle Hank was just turning the cows loose to go to pasture. He had about 11 cows, so we didn't learn all their names. However, it was easy to pick out Francis striding ahead of them. He looked fearsome, and we didn't need reminding to stay clear of him.

As we came back from the pasture, Grandma told us that she had to do her housework and we should entertain ourselves for a while. She pointed to a little building not too far from the house.

"That little shed was originally built as a pigpen, but since we don't raise pigs it just sits empty. I think it would be a nice playhouse for you girls. It will make a nice place to play when the sun is too hot to stay outside."

"Oh, goodie!" we shrieked as we raced toward the building. It was odd looking, as half of it was underground. Years before someone had dug a large hole, then added a wall three or four feet above the ground, and a roof. We stepped down into it and stopped. It was dirty and full of spider webs.

"Go get a broom and rags from Grandma, and I'll get a bucket of water," I directed. We all ran different ways and I got back first. Going down the incline into the building, I stubbed my toe and spilled water all over the floor. Before I could yell a warning, Gertrude came running down the incline, slipped on the wet floor, and fell flat on her back. She looked so funny that I had to laugh, but I knew she could be hurt, so I helped her up. She was very indignant.

"What in the world did you do?" she demanded.

"I spilled the water. What do you think?"

When Grandma saw her muddy clothes, she had a fit. "That clay is so hard to get out of things and you've surely got yourself covered with it."

"Clay?" I exclaimed. "Did you say clay?"

Grandma knew where my mind was running. "Yes, the dirt around here is mostly clay. You can make things out of it like the Indians did. They made pottery and dishes."

Gert changed her clothes in a hurry, and Grandma put the dirty ones in a bucket of water to soak. We were off and running with the clay, making all sorts of dishes, doll furniture, and even "bread," "doughnuts," and "cookies." Working with the clay kept us busy off and on for the rest of the summer.

A few days later Gert came running into the house.

CHAPTER TWO

"Come quick! Uncle Hank is going somewhere on Chum!" I hurried outside to see Chum saddled and tied to a fence post in the front yard. At long last I'd get to see Hank riding this horse that everyone thought was so wild I couldn't ride him.

Soon Hank came strolling over from the barn. He always wore his cowboy hat, but today he had on his chaps and spurs. His lariat was fastened to the saddle. "You kids stand back," he yelled as he untied the horse and led him away from the post.

Placing his left foot in the stirrup, he swung the other one over the horse to land in the saddle. But the second that foot hit the stirrup, Chum went into a spin. He whirled around in a circle, tearing up the ground and raising a lot of dust. But he couldn't throw Hank off. Hank just pulled back hard on the reins, kicked him in the flanks with his spurs, and yelled. Chum reared up on his hind legs, bucked a few times, then shot down the road where Hank wanted him to go. He was wild all right, but Hank could handle him.

Vi turned to me, her eyes frightened. "Do you still think you could ride him?"

Vi wasn't a tomboy like I was and didn't care much for horses, anyway, but I hated to admit failure to her. Nevertheless, I knew deep in my heart that I probably wouldn't ride Chum that summer.

Still, I thought, *I could probably stay on Chum if I hung on to the saddle horn or his mane. But I could never pull back on the reins and kick him in the flanks to straighten him out. Even so, whatever made me think I could ever get up into the saddle in the first place?*

As we walked back to the house, Grandma was standing in the doorway. She had watched the whole thing. Her eyes twinkled at me as I opened the screen door. "Do you still think you could ride Chum?" I gave her a long look. She had known what I was thinking ever since I'd arrived at the farm. I hated knowing that she was right.

"Just because Chum acts tame in the barn where he's tied up doesn't mean he's really tame," Grandma said. "He lets you pet him and feed him because he's tied. But that doesn't mean he can be trusted. Your uncle broke Chum himself, so he knows all his little tricks and naughty ways. If you tried to get on, he'd throw you before you got in the saddle. Then you'd be under his dancing feet."

I shuddered at the thought. "Hank and I want you to have a good time while you're here," Grandma went on. "So don't do things without thinking. When you're around animals, you can't afford to be stupid or dumb. If you kids do what we tell you, you'll get along fine. Besides, how would your parents feel if we let something hurt you?"

Gert was looking out the door. "Hey, there are two big sawhorses out by the barn. Let's make some bridles for them and pretend they're horses and ride them."

We went to the barn and found some twine, which we twisted into bridles. Then we straddled the sawhorses, and pretended we were riding. But my heart wasn't in it. I wanted to ride a real horse, a horse like Chum.

CHAPTER 3

As we played we kept one eye on the lane, watching for Uncle Hank to come home. We had to wait till just before sundown to see that Uncle Hank was still on Chum but leading another horse, a mare. This horse didn't act like she wanted to be led. She kept pulling back and tugging to get away. Then she would run up beside Chum with her ears flattened back, nostrils flaring, eyes wild. I was afraid that she would bite Hank or Chum, but Hank didn't seem concerned.

We started to run out to the road, but Grandma called us back. "You sit right here on the steps to watch. Hank is having enough trouble without your scaring that horse."

We watched quietly as Hank tried to get the horse into the barn. She was scared of the building, for she had never been in one before. Hank rode into the barn on Chum, then, before untying the horse from the saddle horn, he tied him firmly to a post in the barn. Putting Chum in his stall, he then came out to try to get the other horse inside. He took hold of the rope and pulled steadily, all the while talking softly to her.

It took a long time, but he finally got her into the barn, where he led her to a stall and tied her to a post. He put some sweet-smelling hay and oats in the feed box and some water where she could reach it. He closed the barn door tightly so the new horse couldn't get away, even if she managed to break free. At last Hank came into the house for supper. Soaked with sweat, he fell into a chair, exclaiming, "That Kate is a wild one!"

The next morning we kids jumped out of bed the minute we heard Hank's feet hit the floor. We didn't want to miss a single minute of Hank's breaking Kate.

We followed as he strode out to the barn. When he heard us, he turned around and shouted for us to get on top of the chicken coop and stay there. "I'm bringing Kate out here to work with her, and if she gets away from me she could run right over you kids!"

We scrambled to the roof of the chicken house, our hearts beating wildly with excitement. We heard a lot of neighing and squealing in the barn, and after a while Hank came out, leading Kate. As soon as she was in the sunshine and wide-open spaces, she reared up on her hind legs, then slammed down on the ground and ran away.

Hank couldn't hold her. She came flying toward the chicken house, and we sat there, frozen with terror. Just as she got to us, she veered away and went sailing around the house. The yard was fenced, so she couldn't get away, and Hank just let her run. At last she got tired and stopped to rest in a far corner. Hank jumped on Chum, rode over, and lassoed her. Then he led her back and put her inside the corral. That was where he could train her. It was roomy, but there was not so much room that she could run away. He turned her loose and said, "That's enough for one day. We'll leave her in there and let her get used to it."

All day long Kate raced around looking for a hole in the fence so she could escape. Finally she stopped still, her head drooping, the spirit drained from her. As I peeked through the rails at her, I thought, *I think I like her better wild. If I were a wild horse, I wouldn't like to be cooped up like that. I would want to be on the range, running with the herd.* Kate was shiny black and reminded me of the stallion we'd seen the day we came to the ranch.

For the next few days Hank worked with Kate in the corral. At first she'd go crazy for a while, so he would lead her around until she calmed down. He taught her the meaning of "giddyap" and "whoa," by leading her around and starting and stopping when he gave the commands.

Kate was going to be a workhorse, so he didn't try to ride her. After she learned the commands, he had to teach her to wear the reins, and to turn when and where he wanted her to do so. When she had finally learned that, she had to learn to pull things. First Hank tied a small log to her with a rope. It frightened her to have something bumping along behind her, so she ran to get away from it. Uncle Hank was patient and kept slowing her down until she could be driven around the corral, obeying orders and pulling a load.

Next he tried placing a harness on her. He had to tie her to a post to do that, as he knew she would fight having a collar and straps put on her. He'd leave her tied up wearing the harness so she could get used to it and took it off at night.

At last the day came when we sat on the fence watching Hank hitch Kate to Brownie so she could get used to working with another horse. It took two horses to pull farm machinery. Brownie was used to helping Hank break horses, so he stood there patiently while Kate jumped and pulled and tried to break away from him and get out of her harness. But she couldn't budge Brownie, so she finally settled down, and Henry drove the team around and around the corral.

The next day was the big moment. Henry took both horses out of the corral and hitched them to a wagon, then drove off down the lane. Kate was skittish and tried to get away, but with steady old Brownie walking slowly along, there was nothing she could do but walk with him.

He drove up and down the lane for quite a while. Then he went out on the road and drove a ways, hoping they would meet another farmer coming toward them so he could see Kate's reaction.

When Hank came in for supper that night, he looked happy and satisfied. He leaned back in his chair and stretched. "Well, Kate's about ready to go home. She'll make Bob a good workhorse. She has lots of spirit and pep. She'll pull her weight and she's not lazy. Considering how wild she was when I got her, she's turned out to be a pretty good horse."

The next day Uncle Hank took Kate to her new owner. As they went down the lane, Kate trotted obediently along. "Look how nice Kate follows now," Gert exclaimed.

"Yeah, but it was more exciting when she was wild," I said.

Gert scowled at me. "Shame on you."

"I didn't say it was better. I just said it was more exciting."

CHAPTER 4

"This afternoon we're going over to visit our neighbors, Mac and Louise Ritchie," Grandma announced one hot day. "They live only a mile away, so we can walk."

"Do they have any kids?" Vi asked.

"Yes, Donald is about 8 years old, Louise is 6, and then they have twin babies, David and Dorothy." Vi was elated. She loved babies and would really enjoy herself playing with them. I wasn't too happy, myself. Donald was a bit young for me. But Grandma looked at me, her eyes a-twinkle. "They also have a Shetland pony that I'm sure they'll let you ride." That's all it took. I was ready to go.

We started out right after dinner. It was warm and pleasant, and we walked along talking and singing. Suddenly Grandma stood still. "Quiet!" she hissed. "I think I hear something."

Everyone became deathly silent. Then we heard the dry rattle of a snake's tail. We froze in our tracks.

Without moving, Grandma looked around. There, beside a rock, lay a big rattlesnake with a number of wiggly babies. Grandma's voice was quick and quiet. "All of you, stay away from them. Go to the side of the road and bring me some big rocks. But be careful. The father snake might be around someplace."

We kept Grandma supplied with big rocks, and she threw them on top of the snake until it was buried and we didn't hear any more rattles. From then on we stopped singing as we walked and watched the road more closely. We didn't want to run into any more snakes.

As we came into the Ritchies' yard, Grandma called hello and the whole family came running out to meet us. People didn't even have telephones back then, so they got lonely out on those ranches. And since all traveling had to be done on horseback or on foot, people didn't visit all that much, either.

Grandma and Mrs. Ritchie started catching up on the news right away, then they were comparing recipes. I was afraid they'd talk forever. Vi was happy playing with the babies, and Gert seemed content playing with Louise.

I tried to signal Grandma to ask about the Shetland pony, but she didn't even notice. So finally I just asked outright, "Mrs. Ritchie, do you have a pony?"

"Oh, yes." She gave me a big smile. "Donald, take her out and show her our Shetland pony."

"Can I ride him?"

"You surely can."

That's all it took. Donald and I took off at a run.

"His name is Danny," Donald told me. I found out in a hurry that Donald wasn't nearly as young as I'd thought. He

CHAPTER FOUR

knew how to put the bridle and saddle on Danny, and how to cinch the saddle so it wouldn't slide under the pony's belly while racing around the pasture.

Donald took Danny to the watering trough for a long drink. I guess he knew that the pony would be getting a workout, and he did. Around and around the pasture we went, as fast as Danny could go, my dress and hair streaming out behind me. Danny was black, so I pretended he was the black stallion I'd seen and loved so much. Hanging on to Danny for dear life, I pretended that I was riding with a pack of wild horses through canyons and draws. I felt as wild and carefree as I was sure the horses felt, and I enjoyed every minute of it.

Mrs. Ritchie beamed when we finally came back to the little group sitting under shade trees in the front yard. "That was the best afternoon of my entire life," I told her.

The day passed quickly. All too soon it was time to go home. Before we left, Mrs. Ritchie made some cold lemonade with water from a deep well. She brought out some luscious looking apple tarts made from dried apples. The crust was crisp and flaky and the filling sweet and juicy. Licking the last juicy morsels from our fingers, we started for home. We wanted to get back before nightfall. Rattlesnakes couldn't be seen in the dark!

Gert and I were walking a little ahead, and we passed an old run-down barn and house. It was empty and deserted. Suddenly I stopped in my tracks. "Grandma, there's a snake slithering across the road up there, and it stretches from one side to the other."

We all stopped and waited until it crossed the road and vanished into the tall grass on the other side. Then we looked to Grandma to see what she was going to do.

"Oh, we won't hurt him," she told us. "That's a black snake and they're harmless. They're useful, too. They eat the rats and mice that like to eat our grain."

We breathed a sigh of relief and went on. Two snake episodes in one day was a little too much. As we came through our pasture, Hank was just bringing in the cows for milking. We helped him drive them in and told him about visiting the Ritchies, riding the pony, and seeing rattlesnakes and a black snake all in one day.

* * * * *

"I have a job for you kids today," announced Hank at breakfast the next morning.

"What is it?" we asked.

"It's getting the potato bugs off the potato plants. The way they're chewing up the plants, we won't have any potatoes this winter."

"You mean pick them off with our *hands?*" gasped Gert. Viola turned a little pale.

"Oh, you won't have to touch them at all," Hank said. "We have a way of doing it. I'll show you."

When the dishes were done, we all trooped out to the spud patch, as we called it. Grandma came too. Hank gave us each a bucket and a piece of shingle. Then he showed us what to do.

"You lay the bucket sideways beside the plant, then hit the plant lightly with the shingle. The bugs will just pop off into the bucket."

That didn't sound too bad, until he continued, "You may have to hit the plant a few times to get them all, and the stubborn ones you'll have to pick off with your hands. They're nice little bugs. Not at all squishy."

It wasn't that hard once we got started. And as he'd said, they weren't smushy or squishy.

It was a hot, sunny day and the rows were awfully long. Our backs soon ached from all the bending, and we got so thirsty, I thought we'd drink the well dry.

When we finally finished, Grandma was ready for a few minutes rest on the couch before dinner. But Vi had a better idea for us girls. "Uncle Hank, could we have a few potato bugs to play farm with?" she asked him. "We like to play farm, but we need something to use for cows and chickens. We've been using rocks and stones for our animals, but it would be so much more fun if we had a potato bug farm."

Hank looked at her as if she'd lost her mind.

"Oh, can we, can we?" begged Gert and I. "That would be fun!"

He gave us each a handful, but we knew he thought we were strange. "Don't you let a single one get away," he told us. "We didn't do this hot job for nothing. When you get through with your game, you throw every one of them into a bucket so they'll be burned with the rest of the bugs."

We ran to our little playground where we'd had so much fun mixing clay and water to make dishes and tiny buildings. We started building little houses out of clay, making doorways, walls, sheds, and a little fence around it all. We had a time keeping the bugs from crawling over the clay fences, but we didn't let any of them get away.

At last we tired of the game, we gathered up the bugs and tossed them into the burn barrel. We thought that was a cruel way to kill them, but Uncle Hank had said, "In this world it is a constant battle between man and the bugs, and I want to be sure that I win this one."

Then we went in and washed our hands for dinner.

CHAPTER 5

We lived too far from town to go to church on Sabbath, so we had church at home. The Ritchie family would come over to spend Sabbaths with us; without them it would have been a long, lonely day. We weren't allowed to play ordinary games on Sabbath.

Hank had a mouth harp and he played for our song service. We sang from *Christ in Song* and we all knew most of the songs. Often Gert and I sang a duet for Sabbath school. When it was time for the lesson study, Vi studied the lesson with us children. Mr. Ritchie taught the adult lesson, and since we weren't tied to a time schedule, the adult lesson sometimes stretched on forever.

We'd sing some more to begin church, then Mr. Richie would read an article from the *Signs of the Times* or the *Review*, or the adults would just study some subject in the Bible.

After church we ate dinner together. Mrs. Ritchie always brought some food which we put together for a potluck. Both Grandma and Mrs. Ritchie were such good cooks that it was always scrumptious. I think they tried to outdo each other every week.

In the afternoon the adults would visit while we kids would sit on the floor and play with the Ritchie twins. Sometimes Mrs. Ritchie would tell us stories to help fill in the time.

Late in the afternoon they started back home again. There were always cows to milk, eggs to gather, and chickens to feed—even on Sabbath. With no electric lights, we tried to get as much finished before dark as we could. There were kerosene lanterns to use, of course, but they weren't very bright.

One day we were sitting on the front steps in the early-morning sun when Gert happened to look down the lane. "Oh, look, somebody's bringing a horse," she squealed. Sure enough, a man on horseback was leading another mare down the road toward the house.

"I'll bet Hank is going to get to break another horse," I told my sisters

"She doesn't look very wild to me," Vi said. And she didn't. Her head sort of drooped, and she certainly wasn't squealing and jumping around like Kate did when they brought her down the lane.

Hank went out to talk to the man. A few minutes later he untied the horse, grasped the halter rope, and led her toward the barn. The man rode alongside. He knew Hank would need help getting the horse in the barn. They really had a time, too! She was deathly afraid of the building, and they had to pull from the front and hit her from behind before they could get

CHAPTER FIVE

her into the barn and tie her in a stall. Hank gave her some food and water, and left her to get acquainted with her surroundings.

At last Hank came back to the house. "Yes, this is a new horse to break," he told us. "She's terribly frightened around people and buildings, and it's going to take her a while to get over her fear and get used to us." He seemed to look straight at me as he went on. "I don't want you kids to go near the barn or make a lot of noise around there. She's very nervous. When she understands that no one is going to hurt her, I'll be able to work with her."

"What's her name?" Gert asked.

He smiled. "Queenie. But she surely doesn't look or act like one, does she?"

That afternoon we were sitting in our playhouse when we heard the most awful banging noise. We jumped up and ran toward the barn, but Vi called us back. "We're not supposed to go near the barn. You know what Hank said."

I stood up, hands on my hips. "I think we should find out what's going on and tell Hank if it's serious. Let's tiptoe over and peek through the door to see what's going on."

Barn doors are made in two parts so that the bottom can be closed to keep the animals in, while the top is open for air and light. Carefully, quietly, we crept to the barn and peered in the open door. What a terrible sight!

Poor Queenie was pulling back on the rope as tight as she could and banging her head against the two sides of the stall. She was banging it with all her strength, and her neck had been rubbed raw and bleeding from the rough rope.

We felt so sorry for her. It hurt me to see her. So we ran to the field to tell Hank. He just shook his head. "There's no way I can stop her," he told us. "She just has to quit when she gets tired."

All afternoon we cringed as Queenie kept on banging. I wondered how she could keep from killing herself. When Hank finally came in for the evening, he put other horses in the barn and Queenie quieted down a bit. It must have comforted her a bit to have other horses around. We ate dinner. It grew dark. And we could still hear Queenie banging her head against the stall. The sound carried all the way to the house.

Poor Queenie, I thought, I know you want to be as free as the wind and run the range with the other horses. But what will happen to you if you don't stop banging your head to pieces? As I fell asleep, I could still hear the faint banging. I worried myself to sleep, wondering if she might actually kill herself out of fear.

Early the next morning Hank went into the barn and tried to talk calmly and soothingly to Queenie. She just snorted and kept on banging her head. He tried to smear medicine on her wounds, but she tried to bite him. She hadn't eaten a thing since she'd arrived and had only drunk a little water. Hank was worried about her. "I'll wait a few more days. She might calm down yet," I heard him mutter to himself as he went on with his work.

Queenie's neck looked so bad, and I felt terribly sorry for her. I prayed all day that she would get some sense and stop banging her head against the stall. If she would just stop that, her neck might heal.

But one morning we saw Hank on Chum leading Queenie down the road, and we knew he was taking her back home—unbroken.

That night at supper we were all questions. "You could break Kate. Why couldn't you break Queenie?"

"That horse is just plain loco!" he exclaimed. "Some horses just resist learning anything, and if they're still scared of everyone and everything like Queenie was, there isn't much you can do with them. There's a chance that if Queenie was just put out to pasture with the other animals and kept there a long time, she might tame down. But Mr. Benton needs a horse right away. He'll just go get another one and hope for better success.

"I'll bet poor Queenie's glad," I told him. "She can run in the wind and be free again and do as she pleases."

CHAPTER FIVE

"Oh, wild horses do have a pretty good time of it in the summer," Hank said. "There's plenty of prairie grass to eat. But when winter comes, it's a lot harder. We have blizzards around here, and often the snowdrifts are so deep that the horses can hardly wade through them. Packs of wolves and coyotes attack them and eat them, because they're hungry too." He sighed. "Wild horses can be pretty skinny by spring."

He looked around the table. I could feel myself holding my breath, and even Grandma looked interested. "Now, when winter comes, farmers bring their animals into the barn," Hank went on. "There they can be kept warm and fed regularly. They have hay and oats to eat." He threw me a wink. "Oats to a horse are like candy to children. The animals know they are loved, and they don't mind working, either." Hank took a deep breath. That had been a pretty big speech for him.

"Some people are like Queenie," Grandma continued. "They want to run wild. They're never content. They never settle down. The problem is that there is so much to hurt them when they're away from people who love and care for them."

I closed my eyes. I felt warm and loved. But I still couldn't help hoping that Queenie's neck would heal out in the sunshine and fresh air. And I hoped she wouldn't starve to death the next winter out in the snow and storms.

SOWH-3

CHAPTER 6

One morning Gert and I decided to play in the sandpile behind the house. It was cool there in the mornings, and we liked to make farms or play with our dolls in the sand. On that side of the house was a hole that went under part of the house, a crawl space.

I happened to look that direction when a snake came slithering out toward me. I knew it wasn't a rattler. Rattlers are gray, with diamond shapes on the backs, and they coil up to strike. This snake was long and skinny. It didn't coil, but it raised its head and darted its tongue back and forth.

Gert let out a scream. She was so frightened that her voice

rose higher and higher into a little squeak. I wondered if Grandma could hear her. I didn't know what to do, as I'd heard that some snakes would chase you if you ran. If the snake was happy just lying there looking at us, I was too.

Vi heard the terror in Gert's voice, and she and Grandma came running. One look at the snake and Grandma relaxed. "It's just a blue racer," she told me. "It won't hurt you." She stamped her foot, and the snake disappeared under the house again. But somehow the sandpile lost its appeal, and we went somewhere else to play.

As we walked toward the barnyard, I saw a jackrabbit hopping along. "I'm going to catch him," I whispered. I started creeping up on him, but he saw me and leaped away. I ran as fast as I could, but he soon left me in a small cloud of dust. Turning around, I saw that everyone was laughing at me.

"You're a fast runner all right, but when you can outrun a Montana jackrabbit we'll find someplace to let you race where you can earn some money," Grandma said, laughing.

Just then I saw a hen and her chicks in the yard. The hen was clucking wildly and trying to get all the chicks under her wings. Vi looked up into the sky and yelled, "Grandma! A hawk!"

We'd done this before. Grandma waved her apron and all of us started to yell. We grabbed our hats and waved them in the air. And we ran toward the hen because we didn't think the hawk would attack with people near.

We scared away a number of hawks that way, yelling and waving. And if they didn't go away but kept circling, Grandma would get a box, put the hen and her chicks in the box, and put them in the chicken house until the hawk disappeared.

Sometimes if Hank was home, he'd shoot at the hawk with his shotgun. He never hit one. They soared too far away.

Then one day it happened. I was kneeling on the ground in our clay workplace, making little clay dishes. A hen and her chicks were nearby, scratching for bugs. Suddenly something hit the ground with a thud and a flutter of wings. A hawk grabbed a chick and flew away with it. I heard its last frightened "cheep." It scared the wits out of me, and I ran to get Grandma.

"I'd better put her in the chicken house," she said, bustling out with a box and gathering up the little family. "If that hawk got one chick, he'll be back for another."

The sunshine was still bright. The hen and her chicks didn't seem to mind an afternoon in the shade of the chicken house. But I carried a lump in my throat for the rest of the day. I knew the hawk had to eat too. But why did he have to eat one of our little fluffy chicks?

CHAPTER 7

The summer passed all too quickly. Some work, a lot of play and fun, made the time fly. But we still hadn't seen any of our cousins since our first day in Montana. Then one morning Grandma whispered a surprise. "We're going to town tomorrow, and when we come back we'll bring your cousins with us."

I fairly danced with excitement. Besides Aunt Mattie's fair-haired daughter, Isabelle, she was rearing her two orphaned nephews. Dark of hair and eyes, 9-year-old George was fun in a quiet way. But little 6-year-old Albert was something else! He looked like a fat-cheeked little cherub, but he was a real scamp! When he was up to some mischief, his dark eyes just shone. They shone most of the time!

We could hardly wait for the day to pass. Mom had given us a generous allowance for the trip, and so far we hadn't had a chance to spend any of it. So we decided to make a list of the things we'd buy when we got to the store in Wibaux.

One thing I wanted was a big straw hat. The sun brought out freckles on my pale skin, and my face was so peppered with them that you couldn't stick a pin between them.

Sleep came hard that night, but finally I felt myself drifting off, thoughts of the next day filling my mind. We were up with the sun, scurrying around to pack the wagon with things to trade at the store. It was hard to know what to wear. I wanted to look especially nice, but Vi insisted that I wear a dress with sleeves in it. "If you don't, your arms will get all sunburned," she warned me.

But my favorite dress didn't have sleeves. Besides, I didn't think I would burn. My arms were already Indian brown.

Hank brought hay to put in the floor of the wagon and spread a horse blanket over it so we'd have a soft place to sit. Otherwise, we'd be bouncing around on the hard boards all the way to town and back.

The long, hot, dusty trip seemed even longer, because the road wound through so many different farmers' fields. At the entrance to every single field, Hank jumped down from the wagon and ran to open the gate. Grandma drove the horses through, then Hank closed it again. Never, but never, would anyone leave a gate open. There could be livestock in the field, and they would wander away.

These delays made me mad. But I didn't dare say anything. What if someone did that to Hank's cows? But all the stopping and waiting made the trip seem to last forever.

Prairie dogs and coyotes entertained us along the way. We even saw a herd of wild horses far in the distance. I wondered if Queenie was among them. I hated to think of her. She might even be dead, especially if her sores had gotten infected. Poor scared Queenie. She could not learn to obey or become friends with people.

Just about the time I thought we were never going to get there, we saw the town water tower off in the distance. As our wagon lumbered into town, our cousins came running. They'd been watching for us, and the time had passed as slowly for them as it had for me. They climbed into the wagon and rode the rest of the way to their house with us. There were no rubber tires on farm wagons, so Aunt Mattie could hear the squeak of our wheels long before we arrived.

She had dinner ready, of course. She knew how hot and tired we would be. She had a big garden, so we had new potatoes creamed with baby peas and onions. Green salad, other vegetables, homemade bread, and huckleberry pie finished off the meal.

How we ate! Grandma and Aunt Mattie chattered about all the things that had happened since they'd last seen each other. But we couldn't stay long. We had some shopping to do and we had to be home before dark. With a full moon, a person could make it home at night, but no one even wanted to try when the moon wasn't full or the sky was cloudy.

Izzy, George, and Al already had their bags packed. They were as excited as we were. Aunt Mattie fussed to Grandma that she wasn't sure about letting Al go. He was so young and so full of mischief. But Grandma told her that she wouldn't do that to a little kid. Make him stay when the rest of his cousins were going to spend some time together. Poor Grandma. She didn't know what she was getting into.

It didn't take but a minute for us to ride to the general merchandise store. Hank tied the horses to the hitching post and gave them each a drink of water while we kids piled out of the wagon. Our cousins didn't have any money, but that didn't keep them from having fun.

We girls ran to the straw hats. Vi chose a green one, Gert, a blue, and me, a saucy red. We were so proud of them that we paid for them at once and put them right on our heads. Then we went to the candy counter to gaze at its wonderful treasures.

"Oh, licorice whips!" I cried. "I want some."

"Look at those licorice plugs of tobacco and cigars," George said. "We need some of those to play cowboy with. That's what cowboys have!"

"Hank's a cowboy and he doesn't smoke or chew," Gert protested.

"Of course not. He's an Adventist cowboy," Izzy said.

"Well, we'll just be playing. It's just candy." George folded his arms as if he dared us to disagree.

Gert folded her arms too. "What will Grandma say if she sees us with cigars in our mouths? I think she'll hit the roof."

A little grin played around Izzy's mouth. "Let's get them anyway. We'll be playing outside, and she probably won't even see us. If she does, we'll just eat them. After all, they're just candy."

So Gert and I, the kids with the money, each bought a half dozen each of cigars and plugs so we could share with our cousins. Then I got a big bag of gumdrops—my favorite—and Gert bought a bag of her favorites, jawbreakers. She'd suck on a few on the way home and make the rest of them stretch out as far as she could.

While we kids were haggling over the candy, Hank kept himself busy shopping and piling things into the wagon. Grandma and Vi were in a corner of the store, choosing material to use for new aprons. Grandma also bought new cheesecloth. She used it to drain the cheese when she made cottage cheese.

We finally got everything packed into the wagon, and we all jumped in and were on our way. Bum and Brownie knew they were going home, and they just kicked up their heels. Most of the time the wagon was too heavy for them to run with, but every now and then they'd really take off and *go*. We loved their bursts of energy. It made the wagon bounce around, and we'd bounce with it on the straw Hank had put in the back.

Vi sat up on the wagon seat between Hank and Grandma. She was always quiet and good-natured, and Al decided she'd be a good one to tease. He picked up pebbles and seeds from the hay and carefully, gently, put them down the back of her neck.

Vi squealed! She thought a bug had gone down her back.

Grandma jumped too. "What in the world!" she exclaimed.

"Someone put something down my neck," Vi said, jumping and shaking her dress till they all fell out.

Grandma turned around and shook her finger at Al. "You behave yourself," she told him. "Sit still and just watch where we're riding."

Al sat still for about 60 seconds. His hands wriggled and tickled the straw. He looked off in the distance. He twisted around to make a face at Gert. Then oh-so-carefully he crept forward and tickled the back of Vi's neck with a piece of straw.

Vi screamed! Grandma, watching him out of the corner of her eye, moved faster than he did. Her smack sent him sprawling. He wasn't hurt much, but it did settle him down a bit. I felt a little sorry for him. He deserved it, but he was so cute.

The next time I saw him creeping toward Vi, I yelled. Al tossed me a dirty look.

Izzy had a piece of cord and kept herself busy playing "skin the cat." I don't know where it got such a funny name, but the game is played by making different designs on your fingers with the string. Gert and I had never seen it before, so we spent some time watching and learning how to do it.

Finally we started to sing to pass the time. In that part of Montana the wind blows all the time, but sometimes it is really strong. Just as we were starting to enjoy the songs, a strong gust of wind blew my new red hat right off my head. I grabbed for it, but it was gone, flying across the prairie dog town like a tumbleweed.

"Stop, Hank!" I cried. "I have to go get my hat."

He stopped the horses and shaded his eyes. He shook his head. "You could never catch it. That hat's a long ways off and still flying. Besides, you could step on a rattler, running across a patch of ground like that."

Tears streamed down my cheeks as I watched my cherished hat disappear in the distance. I'd wanted that hat. I loved that hat. I'd planned to wear it when we played cowboy. I'd imagined myself throwing it on my head with a flourish, the way Hank did with his.

Hank giddyaped the horses and we started rolling again. "I wonder if a prairie chicken will make a nest in your hat," Izzy wondered aloud.

George giggled. "I'll bet the prairie dogs dived into their holes when they saw that thing coming."

Isabelle tried to comfort me. "I don't have a hat either, so you won't be the only one."

I dug my fist into my eyes to stop the tears. But you didn't *want* one either, I wanted to tell her.

The rest of the ride was uneventful. Even Al had tired and slowed down. When we pulled into the yard, we kids jumped off and ran into the house to put away our things. Then we brought the cows in from the pasture. Hank unloaded the wagon and took the horses to their stalls. Grandma and Vi gathered eggs, then went into the house to fix supper. The rest of us hung around Hank, watching him doing the milking.

I often wondered why Vi stuck with Grandma all summer. I wondered how she could be having fun. Many years later, when I had a granddaughter of my own who liked to do things with me, I finally understood. Vi and Grandma were having a fine vacation together.

CHAPTER 8

The next morning we could hardly wait to make stick horses with binder-twine bridles. We made whips to use on the horses to make them go faster, often striking our own legs through carelessness. We stopped our wild riding now and then to pull out our licorice plug tobacco and take a chaw. We each had a licorice cigar to chew on too. We rode around and through the corral. We dodged cow pies and each other, always keeping out of sight of Grandma and Vi. We knew what *they'd* say if they saw our licorice tobacco!

We found some rope in the barn and tried lassoing each other. All we got out of that were a few bruises. We pretended that we were driving big herds of cows and horses and had a grand time with that for the rest of the morning.

When Grandma called us for lunch, we trooped in, hot and flushed from so much running in the hot sun. "What are you trying to do? Get sunstroke?" Grandma demanded. "Go wash yourself off in the horse trough before you try to eat. And next time stop and rest in the shade now and then."

The cool water felt good on our heads and arms. We came back in, damp and hungry. "Did I see you kids running around with sticks in your mouths?" Grandma asked as we were eating lunch.

George shot me a quick look. I looked down but not before I saw a certain look in Grandma's eyes.

No one spoke. "Well?" Grandma asked.

The kids all looked at me, so I knew I had to answer. "No, it wasn't sticks. We know better than to run with sticks in our mouths." I took a sip of milk. "It was just licorice."

"Hmmm. Licorice cigars, I'll bet. How does it look for Christian children to be running around with cigars in their mouths!"

"Oh, Grandma, it was only a fun game," George spouted. "We didn't mean anything by it. There's no one around to see us anyway."

Gert nodded. "You know we wouldn't think of using real cigars. This is just candy."

"Well, I'm glad to hear it," Grandma told us. "You know, it helps to pledge to God about something like that. Then when temptations come your way, you'll think twice about breaking your pledge."

She gave us a long, serious look. "How about each of you raising your right hand and pledging to Jesus that you won't ever use any kind of tobacco?"

We wriggled a little, but we gladly made the pledge. And we meant it, too. Grandma told us that we could finish our game, but afterward she hoped we'd play that we were cowboys like Uncle Hank.

CHAPTER EIGHT

"We only have one cigar apiece anyway," Izzy said. "We'll save them for tomorrow."

"And one more plug," Al whispered. "But we can hide them in our pockets. No one will see them there." Somehow the next day the tobacco game had lost its zest. We ended up eating the rest of the licorice without much gusto.

After dinner we went back outside, but the noontime sun was too hot. Wondering what to do, we drifted over to some shade. "I wish I had a real horse to ride," I said for the hundredth time that summer. "It's just awful to think that I'll spend a whole summer here and the only riding I got to do was one afternoon at the Ritchies'."

Al brightened. "Maybe we could go over there."

"Naw, not a chance. Grandma wouldn't let us go that far alone. Besides, we saw a rattlesnake on the way."

Izzy leaned forward. "Mom is going to have you kids come spend a week in town with us. And our neighbor boy has a good riding horse. He's sort of reddish brown like a fox, so his name is Fox. And he's real good to ride. I've ridden him and he runs fast."

I gasped and my heart did a little dance. "You mean it?"

"Sure, I mean it. I'm sure he'll let you ride." She frowned, thinking. "But in the meantime, what about Shorty?"

"Who's Shorty?" Gert and I spoke at the same time.

"That old white horse out there in the pasture with the cows. He's 25 years old and can't work anymore. But you can ride him. He's tame and you probably can't get him to go faster than a slow walk."

"Yeah," George exclaimed. "At least he's a real live horse."

We all leaped up and ran to the house. "Grandma! Grandma! Can we ride Shorty?" Why hadn't anyone thought of this before!

Grandma sank into her rocking chair and just laughed. "You want to ride Shorty? Well, he might be a little better than a stick horse. At least he uses his own legs. Do you think you can catch him?" Her eyes twinkled. "Do you think you can catch him? He might be rather wild."

The cousins laughed. "Shorty, wild? We'll be lucky if we can make him move."

"OK," Grandma said. "He's wearing a halter and short rope, so if he lets you get near him, you can catch him all right. Bring him up and put a bridle on him, but don't get one of Hank's saddles. You'll have to ride him bareback."

We were off and running, but Grandma's voice reached out and brought us back. "Watch out for snakes. If you see one, come on home. Don't try to kill it. They can coil and strike from a good distance. And Al, you stay here with me."

"Aw, Grandma."

But we were already gone.

We found Shorty munching away at the dry pasture grass. He looked up and wagged his ears when he saw us but didn't try to run away. Izzy knew horses better than the rest of us, so she walked up slowly to him and began to talk softly.

"Hi, Shorty, old pal, old chum. How about giving us a ride today?" He let her come right up, and she grabbed his rope. A moment later she was headed toward the house. We whooped with victory.

Izzy and I rode him first. Izzy sat in the front and held the reins. There was a long lane from the front of the house down to the road. Grandma said we could ride back and forth on the lane, but we shouldn't get on the road.

With no saddle or stirrups, we had to have him stand by the porch so we could climb on his back. He was patient and didn't seem to mind. Izzy shook the reins, and kicked him in the ribs, and we were off. At first it was kind of scary, way up high with nothing to hold on to but Izzy, but soon I thrilled to the ride of a real live horse!

George and Al went next. Then Izzy went with Gert. Gert wasn't as excited about riding as I was and surely didn't want to try it alone.

Back and forth, back and forth, the horse patiently plodded with his load. I wanted to ride him alone, to see if I could make him run. Coming back up the lane, I started hitting him with the reins and kicking him in the ribs. He actually ran for about six seconds. I was overjoyed! So I tried it again and again. But except for a few seconds, Shorty had only one speed. Slow. He wasn't about to run much on a hot summer afternoon.

When Gert got on him again, he must have known he had a timid rider. He began to limp pitifully, acting as though he were in pain.

"I guess we wore him out," George said. "We'd better turn him loose."

We were all a little scared. Quickly we took off the bridle and put his halter back on. We let him have a long drink at the watering trough. Then we gave him a handful of oats and led him, still limping, back to the pasture. We opened the gate and let him go through.

Instantly Shorty galloped off, with no sign of a limp. We looked at each other, our mouths open in surprise. Then we started giggling and laughing until we couldn't stop. "That old fraud!" I exclaimed. "He was just fooling us all the time."

"Well, I guess he knows how to get out of work," George said. "It sure worked for him."

We rode Shorty every afternoon after that, for as long as our cousins were with us. He'd let us ride for only so long, then would pull his limping trick. We knew he was fooling, but he was old and we'd quit when he let us know he was through.

Sometimes when we let him back into the pasture, it looked as though he turned and laughed at us before he galloped away. He never galloped when we were riding him. Galloping is the smoothest riding there is, but Shorty had his limits.

But at least I got to ride a real live horse on Grandma's Montana farm!

CHAPTER 9

As the days wore on, we all got tired of Al's teasing. Vi especially bore the most of it. Maybe it was because good-natured Vi never tried to get him back. He knew better than to sneak up on one of the rest of us. We'd grab him and make him sorry! His favorite trick was to creep up behind Vi and give her a hard pinch. She'd let out a squeal and Al would laugh his head off. We all knew what had happened when we heard Vi squeal.

Grandma fussed at him but never punished him. Maybe she was too busy keeping her house and chickens and all of us out of big trouble. One evening we were sitting in the living room, singing and listening to Hank play his mouth harp. Quietly Al sneaked up to Vi and gave her a hard pinch.

"Ouch!" she yelled. "That hurt." Tears sprang to her eyes. Grandma made a lunge for Al, but he was too quick for her. He ran from the room and slid under her bed. The bed was low to the floor and he could just scoot under it.

Grandma was right behind him. She stooped down and tried to grab him, but naturally he scooted farther away. She couldn't move the bed away from the wall. It was too heavy.

Grandma must have been desperate. She marched back to the kitchen, picked up three pieces of firewood, and marched back to the bed. Then she stooped over and hurled them, one at a time, under the bed at Al.

"Stop! You'll kill him!" Vi gasped. But we needn't have worried. He was so agile that Grandma couldn't touch him.

At last Grandma straightened and went back into the living room. Hank picked up his mouth organ and began blowing again, but the evening was ruined. That Al! Grandma was pretty patient, but she had a temper.

We spent the rest of the evening ignoring Al. When we all went to bed, he was still hiding. No one knew for sure when he crawled out and got into his own bed. One thing for certain. He waited until he heard Grandma snore.

Many times Hank milked the cows out in the corral. It was lighter out there, cooler and more airy than the barn. All of us children would cluster around him, watching him and playing tag. As soon as he filled a pail with milk, we'd carry it in to Grandma. She'd put it through the milk separator, which separated the milk from the cream.

Grandma made butter and buttermilk out of the cream. Sometimes we drank the cold, tart buttermilk. Often she traded what we didn't need for flour and sugar.

One night while we were playing around Hank and the cows, I saw Al get that look in his eye again. A sly smile crept over his face too, and I knew he was up to no good. He clambered over the top of the corral fence and landed on the ground on the other side. He was gone for a while, and I thought maybe he'd just gone to the bathroom. After a time he came back, a long stick in his hand. He was grinning from ear to ear. A bad sign.

In a corral where you have cows, you also have cow pies. Cow pies are round splats of cow manure. If they're fresh, they're soft and mushy. Al put his stick in the middle of a cow pie, then flipped it, trying to splash it all over us. No one wants to be splashed with that, so Al really had us hopping to keep out of his reach.

I tried to sneak up behind him and grab his stick. But he almost got me in the face, so I didn't try that again. Then he started after me, and I kept running so he couldn't hit me.

I don't know why one of us didn't tell Hank and have him make Al stop. We were a little distance from Hank, and he didn't notice. Without thinking, I ran toward Hank. Al ran too, flipping a cow pie. It hit Hank right in the neck.

We gasped and froze. But not Al. He flew over the corral rails and streaked across the barnyard to the barn.

Hank leaped from the milk stool. It was one of the few times I saw him really angry. He started after Al, then stopped as though he knew where he was headed.

Al had headed for the old pigpen, the playhouse we'd been using all summer. There was only a crawl space to get into it, and Hank knew he couldn't reach Al there. I guess one of us kids could have gone in and tried to drag him out, but none of us wanted to try.

Hank cleaned his neck and went back to milking. When we all trooped into the house for dinner, we told Grandma what had happened. "That kid!" was all she said, but the twinkle went out of her eyes.

When supper was ready, she went and called Al. He didn't come, so we ate without him.

Then the dishes were done and we settled down for fun and games. Sometimes when Hank had done a hard day's work, he went right to bed. He must have been extra tired, because that's what he did that night. When it was about time for us to go to bed, we heard the back door open ever so quietly. Footsteps tiptoed across the kitchen floor. Then a dirty little face peeked into the living room.

"Is Hank in bed?" Al whispered.

We nodded.

Al disappeared in the direction of his bedroom, and that's the last we heard of him that night. Grandma didn't even offer him any supper. I guess she thought an empty stomach might help dampen his mischievous spirit.

Nobody said anything to Al the next morning. I guess he thought Hank had forgotten, but when breakfast was over Grandma shooed us all out the door. All, that is, but Al.

"Young man, you and I are going to have a session," she said sternly.

"Oh, I'll be good today." He flashed her a dazzling smile.

Grandma's hand was quicker than the eye. She grabbed him by the shirt collar and set him down in a chair. From the look on her face, I guess Al decided he'd better listen.

None of us ever found out what went on in the kitchen between Grandma and Al. But when he finally came out to play, he was one subdued little boy. He wasn't cured of his tricks by any means, but for the rest of the time he visited Grandma, his tricks weren't nearly as mean as they had been.

Another thing that tickled Al to no end was the grasshoppers. They were everywhere. Now, in those days girls wore dresses and big baggy bloomers. The grasshoppers would fly up our dresses, scratching our bare backs. We'd run and get someone to help us knock the grasshopper off.

Al was never any help. Of course, with his shirt tucked into his pants, he didn't have trouble with the grasshoppers anyway. I think he would have coaxed them down our backs if he could.

Al is like a wild horse, I thought to myself one evening. He needs someone to teach him to obey and to be considerate of others. He needs to use all his energy for something good instead of always for trouble. I was lying in bed, thinking. I guess it's time for Aunt Mattie to take him in hand. I hope he turns out like Kate instead of like Queenie.

CHAPTER 10

Joy of joys! One afternoon a man came up the lane leading a horse. As usual, Hank and the man had a lot of trouble getting the horse into the barn. When Hank came in for supper, he told us that this horse would be broken for riding. We kids looked at him and squealed. Maybe we'd get to ride him!

Wild horses bucked and did all sorts of things when someone got on their backs. This would be like a rodeo.

Boots, the new horse, was a real beauty. He was shiny black with white fetlocks around his feet and a white spot on his forehead. I longed to pet him but didn't dare. He had big teeth and I knew he might bite. We kids were allowed to go into the barn and be around him, though. He wasn't scared, and it would do him good to get used to people. "Stay away from behind him, though," Hank told us. "He might kick."

The days grew endless. When would Hank decide that Boots was ready to be worked? We thought he'd stay in the barn forever, but finally Hank brought him out to the corral. They'd have a bit of room in the corral, and Boots couldn't run away.

We kids piled up on the corral fence, but Hank waved us down. "Just stand on the ground and watch through the rails. Boots could bite you. Or he could race over and knock you off." So we hopped on down and looked through the rails, ready to take off if Boots got dangerous.

Hank led the horse around the corral so he'd get used to being with him and would learn what he wanted him to do. He'd lead him forward, then have him stop. You don't say giddyap and whoa to a riding horse. You kick him in the ribs when you want him to go and pull back on the reins to stop. Of course, Hank couldn't teach Boots that until he could ride him.

After a few days, Hank tried to get a bridle on Boots. A horse is guided entirely by his bridle. You pull on the right rein and it pulls his head to the right. So the horse turns that way. The same goes for the left side.

But getting a bridle on was something else. Hank had to tie Boots's head close to the rail so he couldn't move around much. Then he put the bridle over his head and ears. Hank put the bit against his lips and pressed, but Boots would not open his mouth. Hank just kept it there and kept pressing. When Boots opened his mouth to squeal, Hank pushed it in and quickly fastened the bridle so he couldn't spit it out.

Boots hated the bit. Hank untied him so he could move his head, then he led him around. He pulled on the right rein when he wanted him to go right. He pulled on the left rein when he wanted him to go left. Later, when Boots was fully tame, he would learn to turn right or left when the reins were laid across that side of his neck. Boots was smart. He learned fast.

This was all very interesting, but we were beginning to get bored. We wanted Hank to start riding Boots. That's when the fun would begin. We didn't have Hank's patience. Hank, on the other hand, wasn't in any hurry to get thrown and have his leg or neck broken. He wanted Boots as tame as possible before jumping on him.

Finally the big day came. We saw Hank coming from the barn with a saddle in his arms. We all ran to our favorite watching posts and even Grandma came out for the show. She was a little scared and wanted to keep her eye on her Hank. We saw Hank as a cowboy, but to Grandma, he was still her son.

First Hank tied Boots's head up. That way a horse can't buck. He also tied him close to the fence so he couldn't move far. It was a job for Hank to get the saddle blanket and saddle on Boots. Boots tried to kick him, push him up against the fence, even step on him. But the horse was on such a short rope that he couldn't do much, and Hank finally got the saddle on him, cinched up tight.

Then Hank turned him loose in the corral. What a sight! Boots bucked and raced around and around the corral. He was trying to rid himself of that frightening burden on his back. Then he came to the fence and tried to rub the saddle off. Of course, it didn't work. He finally stopped, sweaty and exhausted, in one corner of the corral. Hank tied him up again and let him rest. "I'll ride him this afternoon," he told us.

We couldn't wait.

Grandma and Vi fixed dinner in a hurry, and we ate and had the dishes done in a flash. We all trooped down to the corral, where Hank was exercising Boots. He'd already given him a drink and some food.

Finally Hank tied him to the rail again. Then he got on his back and settled himself in the saddle. Poor Boots could only squirm and twist and kick to show his anger. Finally he quieted down. Hank nodded to Grandma.

Grandma went over and untied the rope. Boots was free. Then came the explosion! The moment he felt himself free, he started bucking, running, jumping, and everything else he could think of to rid himself of the awful weight on his back. Around and around the corral he went, with Hank hanging on for dear life. Boots leaped into the air, and came down stiff-legged on all fours. *That* is guaranteed to jar the pudding out of any cowboy, but Hank hung on.

The corral dust grew thick as Boots tore up the ground with his hoofs. At last he went slower and slower. Then he stopped. His sides were heaving and sweat rolled off his body. His breath came in heavy huffs and puffs.

Hank got off his back and tied him to the fence again. Gently he took off the saddle and bridle and walked away with a smile. "We'll try that again later this afternoon," he called over his shoulder.

We knew the show was over for a while. Boots should have been rubbed down after such an ordeal, but he was still too wild for anyone to try it.

For the next few days Hank saddled, bridled, and rode Boots three or four times a day. At last the day came when he opened the corral gate and rode him down the lane. Then he opened the lane gate and took Boots out onto the road. On the road he'd meet other horses and big rumbling farm wagons. He might even meet a car or two. But he had to learn to meet and pass these things without getting scared and bolting away.

Every time Hank got on Boots the horse would buck, prance, and twist around for a while. But Hank would just hang on tight, and soon Boots would calm down and do what Hank asked him to do. One day Hank left on Boots and didn't come back for a long time. We were all a tiny bit worried, but we shouldn't have been. He finally came up the lane; Boots was bringing him home as nicely as Chum ever did.

That night at supper Hank said, "Boots is ready to graduate. I guess I'll take him home tomorrow. He didn't act up a bit today when we started out. I rode him over to his new owner's place, and he rode him too. Boots behaved really well with him, so he's ready to take over." He gave me a little grin. "Boots'll make a good riding horse. It's easy to get him to gallop."

We all hated to see Boots leave. I would have given anything to have taken him for a little ride myself. But we were happy that he was such a smart horse and had tamed so nicely. Again I couldn't help thinking of Queenie. Why couldn't she have been like Boots? The next morning Hank got on Chum and led Boots down the lane, going to his new owner. Boots pranced gracefully along like the champion that he was.

That night I went to bed happy. I was glad that Boots would have a nice warm stall all winter. I didn't want to think about his being out on the cold wild range, with blizzards and wild animals to worry about.

CHAPTER 11

Grandma hummed a little tune as she gathered butter, cream, and eggs together in baskets and boxes. "Are we going to town again?" Gert asked.

Grandma nodded. "Yes. I think we'll take your cousins home tomorrow. They've had a nice vacation, but I bet their mother is getting a little lonesome without them. I need some supplies, too." She bustled around as she talked. "Your parents will be here for a visit one of these days, and I need a few things before they come."

The next morning dawned bright and clear. We ate breakfast and washed the dishes in a hurry, while Uncle Hank fed the chickens and other animals. As he drove the horses and wagon to the front yard, we all grabbed some boxes to help pack the wagon. We were sorry to see our cousins go, but we were excited about going to town again. And we still had a little money burning holes in our pockets!

As we rode along the dusty road, we played guessing games and sang loudly until Hank begged us to stop and give his ears a rest. We'd each brought along a string so we could play "skin the cat" without having to take turns. And as we came to the prairie dog village, George exclaimed, "Esther, do you think we'll see your hat?"

Hank laughed. "With the kind of wind we have around here, that hat is probably in Timbuktu by now." We kids looked and looked, but we didn't see anything red. We did see several bands of wild horses as we circled the hills, and that helped make me happy.

When we arrived in Wibaux, Grandma jumped down from the wagon and went into the post office, even before she took her things to trade at the general store. She came out of the post office waving a letter, a big smile on her face.

We crowded around her as she opened it. It was from Mom.

Dear Ones,

We will be in Wibaux on Monday, August 7. The trainwill arrive at 11:00 a.m. Have someone meet us. We can stay for a week. We can't wait to see you all again. Goodbye till then.

Love,
Mom, Dad, and Bud

Wow! I hadn't been a bit homesick. At least not until Grandma read the letter. It *would* be good to see my folks and little brother again.

The ride back to the ranch went quickly. We talked a mile a minute, going over and over all the things we had to tell our folks and the things we wanted to show them.

The house was already clean, but Grandma had us clean it all over again. She spent hours and hours baking and planning what she'd cook while Mom and Dad were here.

We thought Monday would never come, but of course, it did. We didn't get to go after Mom and Dad, though. We had another aunt and uncle in town, and they owned a nice big car. So they brought our folks and 4-year-old Bud to the ranch.

We knew it would be fairly late when they arrived, but we couldn't help looking down the lane a hundred times, hoping they'd come soon. At last a huge cloud of dust announced that they were almost here. We raced down the lane to open the gate. They rode through, then stopped so we could climb in and ride the rest of the way.

Feeling stiff and cramped from the long ride, Dad and Uncle Harry decided to tour the ranch to limber up their legs. Hank was glad to show them around. He was especially happy to show off Chum. He even offered to let them ride, but they both said no. Uncle Harry preferred his car to a horse, and Dad would rather drive his huge locomotives.

Inside the house Grandma, Aunt Elsie, and Mom chattered away like a flock of starlings. They had several years worth of news to catch up on. Letters just didn't come close to talking face-to-face. In what seemed like no time it had grown dark, we'd all had dinner, and Uncle Harry and Aunt Elsie had gone back to town.

The next morning Hank announced that he had to bundle hay. The hay had been cut and raked into bundles, and he didn't want to take a chance of having it rain.

Mom's eyes fairly danced. "Oh, goody. I want to go too. It's been an awfully long time since I've helped bundle hay."

Dad didn't have any interest in going, however. Like Mom, he grew up on a farm, but he didn't like farm work. "I'll just stay here with Grandma and enjoy my vacation," he told us.

It didn't take long for Hank to come out driving the

hayrack. We all climbed into the rack and Bum and Brownie took us to the hay field. One of us drove from bundle to bundle. Hank threw the bundles of hay up on the hayrack. Mom used a pitchfork to keep the bundles stacked neat and nice. The rest of us kids trampled them down so we could get plenty of hay on the rack.

The rack was about half full when Mom stopped us. "Listen! I think I hear a rattler."

We froze and listened. We couldn't hear anything. Hank picked up the next bundle and threw it up on the rack. Mom picked it up and heaved it back over. There, dropping below the hay, was a big rattlesnake. He hit the ground an instant before the hay did. The hay covered him, but Hank grabbed his pitchfork, dug him out, and killed him. Then he took out his jackknife and cut the rattle from its tail. It had 12 buttons.

Hank tossed the rattle up to me, and I grabbed it with a smile. The kids at home would never believe I'd even seen a rattler, much less helped to kill one. Now I had proof!

From then on, Mom made Hank lift and shake every bundle before he threw it up on the rack. She didn't want any of us trampling rattlesnakes. We didn't want to either.

Finally we filled the rack and started back to the barn. It was fun, riding up there on top of the world. We had to pass in front of the house to get to the barn. The yard in front of the house slanted down into a little hill that went to the lane.

Just then, whatever held the rack to the wagon broke, and the whole thing tipped over. We spilled to the ground, the hay sliding down in an instant, covering us. Hank was able to jump to safety, and he grabbed his pitchfork and started lifting the hay off us.

Dad came running, and grabbed the pitchfork from Hank. "Do you want to stick that thing into them!" he yelled, frightened to death. Grandma rushed out, and the three of them threw hay until we were uncovered. The hay was light. It hadn't packed down tightly and we were just fine. We came up sneezing, brushing the dust from our eyes.

All but Mom. When she tried to get up, her leg gave way.

CHAPTER ELEVEN

Dad and Grandma got her into the house, while Hank jumped on Chum to go call a doctor. He went to a neighbor who had a telephone, and within a couple of hours the doctor came chugging down the lane in his Model-T Ford.

Mom was in terrible pain. The leg was both dislocated and broken, and we kids ran outside so we wouldn't hear her cry. The doctor set her leg the best that he could. There was no hospital in Wibaux, so Dad and Grandma had to help.

This disaster spoiled our vacation. We felt so sorry for Mom. It wasn't fair, but of course, there was nothing to be done about it. We did our best to entertain her and wait on her and keep her company.

We had fun showing Bud the farm, too. We took him to our clay bakery and we all made cookies. Dad actually bought some of them from us. He was always sweet about things like that.

Bud especially liked the sawhorses and spent a lot of time pretending to be a cowboy like Uncle Hank. He wanted to ride a real horse, though, so we took him out to the field and Dad caught Shorty. Bud was scared to ride him alone, so we kids rode with him.

Dad enjoyed a good rest at Grandma's. He carried in wood for her stove and carried out the ashes. He did other chores around the house, but he wasn't interested in helping Hank. And he never did ride Chum.

At the end of the week Dad had to go home alone. He had to get back to his job. The rest of us had to stay until Mom was at least able to walk on crutches. So when Uncle Harry came to get Dad to take him to the train, we moved to town. We'd stay with Aunt Mattie until Mom was well enough to take the long train ride home.

Aunt Mattie settled Mom into the most comfortable place in the house, and the rest of us went to the train station. We were having a lot of fun racing around, playing tag, until we suddenly realized that we wouldn't see Dad for a while. He kissed all of us kids, even the cousins, and gave us all some spending money. Then he grabbed his bags and disappeared

SOWH-5

into the train. He waved out the window to us until the train took him out of sight.

Brushing the tears from our eyes, we looked at the money in our fists and all got the same idea at once—the candy store! The grown-ups went on home and we kids headed for town. We took a long time choosing and bought several different kinds. We didn't hurry home, either. We walked slowly, sharing our candy. We knew our mothers didn't believe we should make pigs of ourselves. And we wanted to have most of the candy eaten before they made us put the rest of it up for later.

CHAPTER 12

The first day we were at Aunt Mattie's, she told us that we kids had to go herd the cows. Being older, Vi could stay home and help take care of Mom.

The town of Wibaux was very small, and lots of families lived on the edge of town so they could keep a cow or two. The cows were pastured on the grassy hills around the village. Some people put their cow on a chain and stake. Others, like our cousins' family, thought that kid labor was pretty cheap. So they had their children take the cow to the hills and stay there to watch it.

Izzy and George weren't too thrilled with the news. They

knew how boring it could be out there all day. But Gert and I were ready for any adventure. We were eager to go. Maybe there'd be other children to play with. At least we could make some stick horses and play cowboy.

When we got there, we found that we were alone except for a number of cows and calves scattered over the hills. We played cowboy for a while, then sat down to rest. I was itching for something to ride, and my eyes wandered from cow to cow. With their bony backbones, they didn't look like fun to ride. But the calves—that could be something else!

"Hey, George," I called, "did you ever ride a calf?"

George looked bewildered. "Why would I ride a calf?"

"I just wondered if it could be done. I dare you to try. If you do, I will too." I looked right at him. "You're smaller than I am, so you go first and see how it works. They look strong enough to hold you."

"Well, I don't know . . ." George paused, a little scared, but interested.

"Come on. Try it just for fun. Izzy and I will catch the calf and hold it. Then Gert can help you on if you need help. You're not scared, are you?"

That did it.

Izzy and I sneaked up on a calf and grabbed it around the neck. George scooted himself onto its back and held on to its neck. Then we let the calf go.

The calf bucked. It kicked up its heels and bucked like a horse. In a couple of seconds George flew over its head, landing on his back with a hard crack. He didn't move.

We all rushed over to him, our hearts in our throats. "Oh, dear Lord, don't let him be dead," I cried. He was white as a bleached sheet and his eyes were closed. He seemed to be gasping for breath.

I've killed him. I've killed him, I thought. *What will Aunt Mattie say? What will happen to me?*

No one moved. We just stood there above him, frozen by fear. Suddenly he took a long breath and started breathing normally again. He opened his eyes, gasping, "What happened?"

My legs felt like jelly. "I guess you had the breath knocked out of you. Are you all right?"

"Can you get up?" his sister asked. "Do you have any broken bones?"

We helped him sit up, and he tried moving his arms and legs. "I guess I'm OK," he said finally. He looked at me with a scowl. "No thanks to you."

The thought of what might have happened sobered us down for a while. We sat on the hillside just being quiet. I hugged my knees and thanked the Lord that George was alive. Clouds filled the vast blue sky. Now and then a cow mooed her pleasure at the grass and sunshine.

"Est," Gert piped up after a while. "What makes you think up so many crazy things for us to do?"

For the first time in my life, I didn't have an answer. The result of my actions laid heavily on my conscience. I knew that I had to use better judgment around these younger kids.

"Are you going to ride one now?" George looked more like his old self, his eyes dancing with mischief. "You said you'd ride one after I did."

I gave a little laugh. "I guess you proved that wasn't such a good idea." I took a deep breath and plunged on. "It was a stupid thing to do, and I'm sorry I teased you into doing it. That wasn't nice. I'd sure get a licking if Mom knew about it, so I hope none of you will tell. I don't want to worry her, since she's still sick."

I think Mom guessed that we were getting tired of herding cows, because she sent Vi to town to get a chain and stake. Mom never did like to have us out of her sight, and for once we were glad of it.

For some time after that, whenever George wanted to play something that I didn't, he'd roll his eyes and say, "I could tell your mother what happened out on the hill." For the rest of the summer we ended up playing lots of things that George liked.

* * * * *

Wibaux is in eastern Montana, about 20 miles from the North Dakota border, and during the summer it is common to have bad thunderstorms. These thunder and lightning shows really scared us. We'd heard of several people who were struck by lightning. I was brave, but I wasn't *that* brave.

One farmer was working a distance from his house when he saw the storm clouds gathering. He thought he had time to make it home, but he didn't. They said that if he'd unhitched a horse and ridden it for all it was worth, he would have made it to safety before the storm hit. Instead, he tried driving the horses in. Lightning struck, and he and his horses were killed.

One woman, thinking the storm was over, stepped out her back door to see if the wind had done much damage. An instant later lightning struck her, and she was killed.

One day Aunt Mattie had a couple of men working in her garden. A storm roared up in the middle of the afternoon, and we all hurried to the house. During a storm we usually huddled in the same room, cringing at the thunder and lightning. These two men were unafraid, however. They sat by a window, watching the town water tower swaying in the wind. "It's a wonder it doesn't fall over," one of them called to us. "It's swaying a foot each way."

At that, we all rushed to the window. The electric light switch was by the door, and several of us stood next to it, looking out the glass.

Suddenly there was a terrible bang. Aunt Mattie, George, and Vi were knocked to the floor. The lightning had come through the switch by the door. Vi said she saw a ball of fire streak past her and go out through the kitchen.

It didn't kill anyone, but Aunt Mattie was stunned. She kept saying, "Bury me in the ground. Bury me in the ground." It didn't make any sense, but finally the men ran out with a dishpan and brought it back full of dirt. Aunt Mattie buried her feet in it. It probably didn't help, but she finally began to feel better. She said she'd heard that if a person was struck by lightning, putting them in the ground would draw the electricity from their body.

Vi and George weren't hurt as badly as Aunt Mattie. And surprisingly, the house didn't catch on fire. After that, we stayed away from windows and light switches during a bad storm.

On an afternoon some days later, those old dark clouds began boiling in from the west. How we hated to see them. Soon the lightning flashes were bolder and closer, the thunder louder. We huddled in the living room, praying.

Then Aunt Mattie had an idea. "The Armstrongs, next door, have a storm cellar. Let's see if they'll let us go down into it."

We kids ran over as fast as possible. Mom came on her crutches, Aunt Mattie helping. The Armstrongs were just getting ready to go into the cellar themselves and were glad to help us. They'd heard what had happened during the last storm.

Mrs. Armstrong had brought some milk and cookies, which she passed out as soon as her husband lit the lamp. The lamp sputtered and didn't give much light, but it was still better than sitting there in pitch darkness. The cookies made it seem like a picnic.

The grown-ups visited for a while. Then we sang some songs and played some guessing games. After a time Mr. Armstrong lifted the little wooden door and peered out to see if the storm had passed. Sunlight streamed down the steps into the darkness, and we all scrambled out.

We saw several tornadoes that summer, but they didn't touch down anywhere near us. That ugly, twisting funnel is terribly frightening if it's coming toward you. Most of the time though, we didn't think of storms. We just did the few jobs that Aunt Mattie required and spent the rest of the time playing in the sunshine.

CHAPTER 13

There was a little hill in our cousins' backyard, and in the side of the hill was a small cave. I don't know who made it or why. It was too small to be a storm cellar, but it was big enough for us kids to crawl inside and play.

One day George found an old worn-out belt as we roamed around the hills. He picked it up and swung it around his head. It had a faded diamond-shaped design. "It sort of looks like a rattlesnake hide, only it's brown instead of gray," I told him.

He squinted in the sunshine. "Yup, it does, doesn't it!"

"Let's have some fun," I told him. "Let's put it in the cave and put my rattlesnake rattle on the end of it. Then we'll see if we can scare the other kids."

I didn't have to tell George a second time. "What'll we do for a head? Without a head it won't look like a real snake."

"Oh, we can set it in a pail and then have the snake going around the pail. His head will be in the back of it and the tail with the rattles will be in front." I had an answer for everything.

We ran to the porch and grabbed a pail. Then we placed it upside down just inside the cave. We draped the belt around it, and I raced to the house for my prize rattles. It only took a moment to fasten the rattles to the end. At first glance, it looked like a real rattlesnake.

We giggled like two thieves, then sauntered back to the house. "Hey, Izzy, Al, come quick! We have something to show you." We knew better than to try to fool Vi. She wasn't any fun.

They came tumbling out the back door, all eager for excitement. "Just come look. We've got something to show you," George said.

"Now be quiet," I added.

We all tiptoed to the mouth of the cave, and George and I pointed inside. The kids came close and peered in. Then they backed out and went flying back to the house.

This wasn't what we'd had in mind. "Stop! Wait a minute," I yelled. "I'm not afraid of it. Just see."

I picked up the "snake" by the tail and took off after them. They screamed at the top of their voices and ran faster. Aunt Mattie and Vi ran out to meet them, with Mom hobbling behind on her crutches.

"Esther's got a rattlesnake!" they yelled.

By this time George and I had stopped running and were trying to hide the evidence. But Mom demanded to know what was going on. At last I held up the belt. "See, it's just an old belt. It was just a joke."

Mom and Aunt Mattie didn't think it was funny. They made George and I come in and sit down for a couple of hours. "Maybe now we'll have a little peace and quiet," I heard Aunt Mattie mutter.

I looked over at George. "It wasn't such a good idea," I mouthed at him.

He mouthed back, "As usual!"

* * * * *

It was hot. I lay on the couch, reading and trying to ignore the bothersome flies that buzzed against the screen door. Just as my heavy eyelids were closing, Izzy came running in.

"I just came down the street and saw Don Debiltson in his yard. Let's go over and see if he'll let us ride Fox."

I leaped off the couch, took a quick look at my dress to see if I was presentable, and we took off. Don lived about three blocks away, right on the edge of town so they could have a stable for their horses and cow.

We found Don in the stable, shoveling manure and spreading hay. Fox and Blaze, their two horses, were in their stalls. Hearing us coming, Don looked up and smiled. "Hi, Isabelle. What are you doing this afternoon?" I think he had an idea what we wanted.

Don wore blue jeans, a cotton shirt, and cowboy boots. Most young men who lived in Montana dressed the same way. Cowboys or not, they wanted to look like them. He had tossed his straw hat down on a bale of hay, and his curly blond hair was damp with sweat. He was a cheerful, good looking guy.

Izzy dimpled up at him. "This is my cousin Esther. She's from Minnesota and has been dying to ride a good horse ever since she got here. I wondered if you'd let us ride Fox for a while."

Don leaned on his fork. "I'm sure Fox could use the exercise. I haven't been able to ride him for a few days. Does she know how to ride a horse?" He looked at me with a knowing expression. His eyes said, *She's just a greenhorn from the city!*

"Oh, yes," Izzy told him. "She's ridden horses before. But

Uncle Hank only has one riding horse, and he's sort of wild. Hank wouldn't let her ride him. Besides, Fox isn't wild. We'll just take turns riding him up and down the road."

"Oh, you won't have to do that," Don said. "I'm sure my brother won't mind if you take Blaze out for a while too. That way you can both take a nice ride together.

Fox had a rusty red coat, just like a fox. He was long-legged and lean, a real riding horse. It would be such a pleasure to sit on his back. His mane and tail were dark brown, and I thought he was beautiful. Blaze was shiny black with a big white spot on his forehead and white forelocks. The Debiltsons really knew how to pick their horses!

Our eyes shone as we watched Don saddle the horses. We were glad that we didn't have to ride bareback. That can be hard on you if you go any distance.

We decided to ride out to the country, and what a ride it was. The day was hot and sunny, the horses fresh and willing to run. At first we made them gallop, as that's the smoothest riding in the world. Trotting jars you up and down and makes your legs raw if you're not wearing chaps, as the cowboys do to protect their legs. Of course, cowboys know how to stand up in the stirrups, but greenhorns like Izzy and me just rode—that's all.

We came to a prairie dog town and rode right over to it for a really good look. I'd wanted to see one up close since the first time we'd passed them, going to the ranch. Of course, the doggies disappeared into their holes as soon as we came their way, but their curiosity got the best of them. One by one their little heads came peeking out of their holes. They gave us a good looking over. They were so cute. Just like fat little puppies.

We didn't see any rattlers. But we weren't afraid as long as we were up on our horses.

When we decided to go back, we let the horses walk for a while. We planned something really fun to end our ride. When we got a half mile from home, we'd have a race to see which horse was truly the fastest. Izzy liked Fox best, but she let me ride him as she wanted me to have the experience. She knew how badly I wanted to tell my friends at home about the ride.

A half mile from Don's, we stopped the horses and let them rest for a while. We petted their necks and talked to each other. I thought that I never wanted to get off my horse.

But finally we knew we had to get back. "One! Two! Three!" I counted. "GO!"

We were off, and we flew like the wind. Both horses were fast, and the wind blew our hair back as we hung on for dear life. Izzy was a little ahead of me, and I kicked Fox in the ribs to make him catch up and pass Blaze.

Just then Blaze saw a big piece of crumpled paper beside the road. He spooked. Stopped dead in his tracks. Izzy flew over his head and landed on her feet. I saw it all as I flashed by.

Pulling Fox to a quick stop, I turned quickly and went back to my cousin. "What happened?"

Izzy stood in front of Blaze, the reins in her hands. She had a dazed look on her face.

"What happened? I can't believe you landed on your feet! You could have broken your neck!"

"That piece of paper spooked him. I never had anything like this happen to me before." She was trembling. "I can't believe I landed on my feet, either. What a feeling."

Izzy climbed back on Blaze and we went on home. Slower.

When we got to the stable, Don was gone and the stable was nice and clean. He saw us come in and came out to help us put the horses away.

He tied each of them in their stalls, took off their saddles and bridles, and threw us a big rag. Izzy showed me how to rub down the horses, wiping off the dust and sweat. Then Don gave us brushes and curry combs. When we finished brushing and combing them, their coats shone. Then we took them to the watering trough. It's not good to let them have a lot of water when they're hot and sweaty.

We thanked Don again and again for letting us ride. On the way home I sang his praises for giving me one of the best days of my life. Izzy agreed. "I just wish he were 10 years old, or that I were 18," she said. "Then I'd like him for a boyfriend."

Horses were more important to me than boys. I gave her a strange look and walked on.

All we could talk about that evening were Fox and Blaze. Aunt Mattie and Mom were glad when we went to bed, to dream, we hoped, of riding horseback and winning the race.

CHAPTER 14

One noon we were all eating dinner when, off in the distance, we heard singing. "Showers of blessings, showers of blessing we need . . ." We all smiled.

"Here comes Lyman," Al said.

Lyman was the tiny son of Aunt Elsie and Uncle Harry. He was about 3 or 4 years old. His skin was white—he never tanned—and his pale-blond hair was sun-bleached until it was white too. Lyman's grandmother lived at the foot of the hill. Aunt Mattie lived on top of the hill. Aunt Elsie lived down the block a ways, and often she'd let Lyman walk over to see his grandmother. As he walked down the street, he always sang at the top of his voice.

"Can we go play with him?" Izzy asked.

"You finish dinner first," her mother told her. "And even then, you wait awhile. Let his grandma have him all by herself for a while. I'm not sure she wants all of you kids in her little house. You can go down and play in her front yard if she'll let you."

Later we all filed quietly into Grandma McKenzie's front yard. Vi went to the door and knocked. "Can we play with Lyman for a while?" she asked.

"Oh, surely," his grandmother said. "Lyman, come see who's here to play with you."

We were always amazed at how grown-up Lyman talked. He seemed so wise for such a little boy. We liked to hear him sing and kept him busy at that.

We had to play baby games with him, like "drop the handkerchief." Of course, we let him win most of the time. But we still liked playing with him.

We were all sitting in a circle on the grass, listening to Lyman sing when his mother came walking into the yard. "I wondered why he was so late coming home. No wonder he lost track of time with all you children to play with."

Lyman jumped up and ran to her. "Oh, Mom, can I stay a little longer. Can I please?"

Aunt Elsie picked him up and gave him a big hug and kiss. "I'll go on up the hill and visit a bit with Aunt Mattie and Aunt Edith. But then we'll have to go home and get supper ready for Daddy."

He wriggled out of her arms and ran back to the circle. We were ready to play again.

Grandma McKenzie came out about then with a plateful of homemade cookies. Games were forgotten as we enjoyed the treat.

After a bit Aunt Elsie came back after Lyman. She took his little hand and the two of them started for home, and so did we. All the way back up the hill to our house, we could hear

C H A P T E R F O U R T E E N

"Showers of Blessings" as long as it took Lyman to get home.

* * * * *

Gert, Izzy, George, and I sat on the front porch. We were bored and trying to think of something fun to do. We'd spent the morning picking potato bugs from Aunt Mattie's potato patch. It had been a long, hot job. We'd played potato bug farm, but now we wanted a little action.

"Let's go for a walk. Maybe we can find some kids to play ball with or something," George suggested.

That would beat sitting around doing nothing. So we trooped in to ask permission to go.

"Don't go too far and don't stay too long," Mom cautioned. She never wanted us out of her sight. Mothers!

"We'll stop at the post office and get the mail if there's any when the afternoon train comes in," Izzy called as we took off.

There was no home mail delivery in Wibaux. Every day two trains came through, one in the morning and one in the afternoon. The post office was a busy place because that's where everyone went to get their mail. Teens went there to meet friends and make dates. Older people went for a little gossip or news.

We started down the street toward town but didn't see anyone to play with or anything exciting to do. Then George saw some children on the north side of town, herding cows. We decided to go up and play with them. They were happy to see us because they were as bored as we. We played every kind of tag we could think of, then flung ourselves down on the ground to rest.

Knowing my mother, I knew it was about time for us to start back. However, we had to pass the stockyards by the railroad tracks. The stockyards consisted of four or five corrals built together. Farmers took their livestock to the train to be shipped to packinghouses. The animals were kept in the stockyards until they could be put on a train.

As we went past, we could hear squealing and grunting,

SOWH-6

so we decided to go over and see what was in the pens. The pens were full of big fat pigs. We climbed up on the top rails to watch them.

"I wonder who owns them," George said.

"I should think they'd be afraid someone would steal them while they're gone. Some people do eat pig meat, you know," I told him.

"Oh, I don't think there are any pig rustlers around here," Izzy said with a laugh. "Their owners are probably just off getting something to eat or making arrangements for a hotel to stay in until the train arrives."

I kept watching those big pigs rooting and running around. Suddenly I had a bright idea. "You know, I'll bet we could ride one of those big pigs. I think it would be fun."

"Now, Esther," George protested, "you know what happened with the calves."

I shrugged. "Look how close to the ground they are. If we did fall off, we wouldn't hurt ourselves. Come on, I'll go first."

I jumped down into the pen, picked a big lady pig, and jumped on her back. My legs were so long that I had to hold them straight out above the ground. I had nothing to hold onto but its ears, and I held on for dear life. The pig went running and squealing all around the corral, chasing all the other pigs before it. When nothing bad happened to me, the other kids leaped down, and we had a great time riding those pigs.

Finally Gert brought us back to earth. "It's getting late," she said, looking at the sun. "We'd better get home or we're gonna get it from Mom."

We looked at ourselves. We were hot and dirty, and we wondered what kind of reception we'd get when we walked in. No matter what, it had been an exciting afternoon.

I hadn't intended to tell Mom about our pig riding. But George was so excited about it that he couldn't wait to tell Al. Naturally, Mom and Aunt Mattie overheard the whole thing.

They called us all in. "What's this we hear about you riding pigs in the stockyards?"

CHAPTER FOURTEEN

We girls looked accusingly at George. "I didn't tell. I didn't!" he shouted.

"We overheard him telling Al about it," Mom said. "Don't you know that those big boars and even some of the sows could have killed you? They've been known to injure grown-ups."

"But they acted scared of us," we cried.

"Don't you remember that big old sow that Aunt Millie had, and how we wouldn't let you go anywhere near her because she was so dangerous?" Aunt Mattie demanded.

We all remembered. We had just forgotten for the afternoon. We stood there like dummies, looking at our toes.

"I don't know why you can't think a little before you do these things," Mom moaned. "We can't let you out of our sight." She stopped, and a horrified look came over her face. "Lift up your dresses!"

We looked at her as though she had lost her mind.

"Lift up your dresses!" she commanded again. We lifted them a little ways, and she let out a yell. "Just look at your white underwear. It's *black!*"

We bent down and looked. Our underwear surely was black. Black from the dirty pigs we'd ridden.

Mom sighed. "I can see what your punishment is going to be. You girls go in and take a bath, then bring your panties out here."

We obeyed. When we came back, we found that Aunt Mattie had taken out a tub and filled it with hot sudsy water. There was a washboard in the tub, too. In an instant we knew what we had to do—wash the black underwear until it was white again. We started scrubbing while George stood by the door, laughing. His overalls didn't get black from the dirty pigs, or at least it didn't show.

Aunt Mattie saw him laughing and had a few words for him. "When the girls finish washing, you are to take the dirty water to the garden and water some of the plants. They need a good drink. After all, you rode the pigs too!"

George's smile faded. We scrubbed and scrubbed, but our

underwear never looked the same again. At least not until we got home and Mom boiled them with strong soap.

Ever since we'd come to stay at Aunt Mattie's house, Mom had been taking little walks on her crutches. At first she could get only as far as Mrs. McKenzie's house at the bottom of the hill. Then she'd rest awhile before coming back up. Each day she went a little farther, until one day she came in, her face wreathed in smiles. "I walked clear to Aunt Elsie's house, visited with her a little while, and came home. And I'm not even tired! I think we can get ready to go home."

We all cheered, but with mixed emotions. We liked being there with our cousins. But it would still be nice to get back to Daddy and our own home and friends.

"Get all your dirty clothes together so we can wash them. We'll get everything clean and ready to go," Mom told us.

Aunt Mattie sent a note to Grandma and Hank by the mailman. So they came in the next day for a last visit with us. Aunt Mattie and Aunt Elsie fixed a big dinner, and of course, Grandma brought her famous sweet-cream cake with the cream frosting and some of her scrumptious cucumber pickles. She also brought fresh deviled eggs.

It all smelled so good that we children kept wandering into the kitchen, wanting to know when dinner would be ready. Finally Aunt Mattie scooted us out and told us to stay away till we were called.

That sent us scampering to the front porch, where we could still smell the good scents but not get in the way. "Let's play something so the time will go faster," Izzy suggested.

" 'Drop the handkerchief,' " Lyman cried, jumping off the porch.

"Don't you think it's kind of hot for a running game?" Gert asked.

"No, no, let's play 'drop the handkerchief.' "

"All right," Izzy told him. "We'll play that for a while. Then you'll have to sing for us."

We were hot and sweaty when Aunt Elsie stuck her head out the door. "Hey, you're going to get overheated, running around in that sun. And Lyman sunburns so badly too. Just sit in the shade. It won't be long now."

We were only too glad to quit. We sat down on the grass under a tree and had Lyman sing for us until we heard the call we'd been waiting for. "Dinner's ready!"

Back in those days, when there was a big crowd, children usually didn't get to eat until the grown-ups were finished. I didn't think much of that idea, and neither did Mom. If there wasn't enough room at the table, she would let us fill our plates and go sit in the kitchen or on the porch. That way we got to eat while the food was hot and plentiful.

There were 13 of us that day, with Uncle Harry and Grandma McKenzie. We couldn't all get around the table, but we didn't care. We kids got to talk more if we weren't eating with the adults. So we ate at the kitchen table and had a wonderful time. Even Lyman got to eat with us, and that made him think he was really big.

CHAPTER 15

The next day was a scramble as we packed suitcases and made a lunch to take with us for our long trip. Our train had no dining car, and we'd be riding all night and into the next day. Uncle Harry came in his car to take us to the station, as it was too far for Mom to walk on her crutches. Izzy, George, and Al ran ahead to the station, as there wasn't room in the car for all of us.

When the train came puffing into the station, we quickly said goodbye. We kids wanted to be first on the train because we wanted to get a window seat. It took Mom a little longer to get her crutches up the train steps.

While we were waiting, we opened the window and talked to our cousins. Soon we felt ourselves moving. Hanging out the windows, we waved and called goodbye until we couldn't see them any longer.

I settled myself by the window, my eyes fixed on the scenery flashing by. I wanted to see at least one more herd of wild horses.

Wibaux was a small town, with little work for men with families. So Uncle Bert, Aunt Mattie's husband, worked summers in different cities, wherever he could find a job. This summer he was in Bismarck, North Dakota, and our train would go through Bismarck about 5:00 in the morning.

Aunt Mattie had written to him, telling him that we were coming through, so he came to the station to see us. We kids were asleep when he got on the train, but Mom woke us up. He gave us each a little bag of candy, talked to Mom until the train started moving, then raced down the aisle and down the steps.

Mom warned us not to eat any candy before breakfast, but she didn't actually forbid it. It was so tempting. When I thought she wasn't looking, I dug into my sack and ate several pieces. Mom was right. I got the worst stomachache of my life. I didn't even want any of the fruit and sandwiches that she brought out a few minutes later.

The train stopped fairly often. That kept things interesting, even though, of course, it really slowed us down. At just about every stop a man would get on the train with a tray hanging around his neck. The tray held Cracker Jacks, gum, fruit, and sandwiches. We always begged for Cracker Jacks because of the toys in the boxes, but Mom let each of us buy only one thing. Everything cost three times as much as it would in a store, and Mom didn't see any reason to waste her money.

When the train finally puffed into our home station, we were so happy we could only jump up and down. The porter got our suitcases off the train and helped Mom down too. We carried the suitcases into the station, where Mom checked them until we could come back and get them.

There were no taxis in our little town, and few people had cars, so we had to walk home. It wasn't very far and we took it slowly, holding back to walk with Mom. As soon as we got into the house, she checked the cupboards and ice box to see what we needed. Handing a list to Gert and I, she told us to take our coaster wagon and bring the suitcases, too.

It was fun walking into town. We saw a dozen kids who knew we'd been away and wanted to stop and talk. But we told them all, "Later, we've got to get stuff for Mom." We had a lot to tell and surely didn't want to have to hurry the telling. Besides, we were starving for a good hot meal. Snacking for a couple of days on the train wasn't like really eating.

First we went to the station and got our suitcases, then to the grocery store. When we got home, we emptied our suitcases and got cleaned up while Mom fixed supper.

As we took our familiar places around the table, it felt good to be home. We bowed our heads and thanked the Lord for a nice summer vacation and a safe trip home.

CHAPTER 16

Minnesota is just as bad about having fierce storms as Montana, and it wasn't long before dark clouds boiled in from the west and covered the sun. We kids came running home from where we'd been playing. We liked to be with Mom when a storm struck.

The lightning blazed, the thunder crashed, and we closed our eyes, our hands over our ears. Rain came down in bucketfuls, and as usual, I was a little scared. The only good thing about a storm was the puddles left afterward. Mom would let us put on old clothes and go wading in the puddles. She always told us to stay out of ditches, however, as they could have broken glass or cans hidden in the bottom.

Finally the storm moved on, and the sun came out hot and bright. Gert and I ran outside to see if there were any puddles. The ground was covered with them and the ditches were full too. We came back inside to put on our old clothes. Our little brother, Bud, came too.

The neighbor children, hearing us yelling and laughing, were soon out wading with us. "I know," I cried, "let's play wild horses. I'll be the leader and all of you follow me and do what I do."

We'd been telling the children about Montana's wild horses, so they were intrigued and eager to play. I led them through the largest puddles I could find, and the mud splashed high. We knew we'd have to hose off in our yard before we could go back home, but that didn't matter.

Then I came to the end of a street and saw a ditch full of water. It looked deep—and exciting! We could really get wet in water like that. Our little town had neither a pond nor a swimming pool, but this ditch would be almost as good.

"Let's try this and really have some fun," I called as I stepped into the ditch. The water was over my knees as I joyfully went splashing through it.

Gert stopped. "You know what Mom said," she sputtered, running alongside the ditch. But I was having too much fun to listen. The rest of the children stepped in and started following me. Some even ducked down into the water up to their necks. We were a muddy, drippy mess.

Suddenly I let out a yell. I'd stepped on something and it hurt! I held out my hand for the others to stop, then crawled out on the bank and sat down. Swishing my foot in the water to wash off the mud, I saw blood streaming from a cut between my big toe and my second toe. It hurt too!

Peering over my shoulder, Gert let out a yelp. "Oh, Esther. What's Mom going to say?"

I gave her a dirty look. "I'm not going home."

"Well, you can't stay here and bleed to death."

I shrugged. Why not? The neighborhood kids clustered

around me, offering useless advice. At last I screwed up my courage, got up, and started hobbling home, walking on the outside of my foot. Gert and I hosed off outside. Then we slipped into our back porch and stripped off our wet clothes. I was wondering how I could make it from the porch to the bathroom without dripping blood all over the floor or letting Mom find out, but Gert took care of that.

As soon as she shed her wet clothes, she went flying through the house to find Mom. "Est cut her foot! Est cut her foot!" she called, and Mom came running.

When she saw the deep cut, she sat me on a chair and got a basin of water. "This has got to be washed clean," she said, "after your wading in all that mud. Of course, the blood has probably washed away the germs." She shook her head. "If it doesn't stop bleeding, we'll have to call the doctor and get some stitches in it."

Finally the cut stopped bleeding but it started up again every time I stepped on it. At last Mom bandaged it tightly and told me to go get dressed. Then she told me to sit down and stay there, unless I absolutely had to go to the bathroom. She would let me hobble into the dining room to eat.

The neighborhood kids came trooping in to see my bandages, but that didn't interest them for long. They soon ran back outside to play, leaving me inside listening to their shouts of fun.

I thought my foot would heal overnight, but the next morning I still had an open cut that hurt too bad to place any weight on it. I tried to force myself to walk, ignoring the pain, but that didn't work, either. Mom changed the bandage after breakfast, putting peroxide and iodine on it. She just shook her head. "You're going to stay off this foot until it heals," she told me firmly. "This is a deep cut, and since it's in your foot, it could easily get infected."

I was doomed to spend another day in the chair. It was awful. I kept wondering when Mom was going to bawl me out for running through the ditch. She wasn't dumb. She knew where I'd gotten that cut.

I was so bored, and it got worse and worse. Gert came running in about midmorning. "We're all going down to Mary's house to run through the sprinkler," she told me. "Her mother's baking cookies and she always gives us some."

Up until then I'd been pretty brave, but that was the last straw. I couldn't help crying at that. I wanted Mom to let Gert pull me in the coaster wagon, but she wouldn't hear of it.

I loved to read and did a lot of it, but after two days I wanted to get up and moving. At the end of the second day, I sat staring out the window, my cheeks wet with tears.

About that time Mom came in and picked up her crocheting. She sat down in the rocking chair and began working on her afghan. "When you told me about your visit to Grandma's, I thought you'd learned some important lessons this summer," she said after a few minutes. "I thought you wanted to be like Kate and Boots, not like Queenie."

"I do," I exclaimed.

"Well, you're surely acting more like Queenie. Banging your head against the stall instead of listening to the advice of those who are older and know better. It's your own fault, Esther, that you're having to miss out on all the fun. I can't let you run around with that bad foot. You might get an infection in it, or even lose your toe."

I rubbed my eyes and looked away, but she went on softly. "You're not a little girl anymore. It's time you realized that you're responsible for all the things you do. You led the whole group of kids into the ditch. What if one of them had been hurt too? You have a big influence over your younger friends and over Gert and Bud. When you lead them into disobeying, you have to answer to Jesus." She sighed and reached across to put her hand on my arm. "It's time you forget about wild horses and try being a tame little girl."

I'd been thinking the same thoughts all afternoon. I'd never forget poor Queenie and how bad I felt because she kept hurting herself. I gazed down the street where I knew the other kids were playing. "I guess wild horses aren't so important after all," I said. "Maybe horses—and people—need to be tame too."

But as I shut my eyes, I could see again the Montana hills and the band of horses running through them. Their tails and manes streamed behind them in the wind. I knew that the very thought of wild horses would always bring a tug to my heart.